A T

STRANGE NEW GOSPELS

THE UNIVERSITY OF CHICAGO PRESS
CHICAGO, ILLINOIS

———

THE BAKER & TAYLOR COMPANY
NEW YORK
THE CAMBRIDGE UNIVERSITY PRESS
LONDON
THE MARUZEN-KABUSHIKI-KAISHA
TOKYO, OSAKA, KYOTO, FUKUOKA, SENDAI
THE COMMERCIAL PRESS, LIMITED
SHANGHAI

STRANGE NEW GOSPELS

By

EDGAR J. GOODSPEED

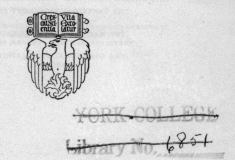

THE UNIVERSITY OF CHICAGO PRESS
CHICAGO · ILLINOIS

TO LOUISE
COMRADE AND GUIDE
TO HAPPY FELLOWSHIPS
AND FAR HORIZONS

PREFACE

FOR many years I have been engaged in
the study of early Christian literature, a
field in which the genuineness of every
document must be rigorously investigated. In
the course of this study there have come to
my attention, from time to time, from obscure
private sources, very interesting, to be genuine documents and Christian antiquity. It was
inevitable that I should in the early test these
stray pieces by the same tests that we constantly apply to all other documents supposed
by ancient. In fact anyone familiar with any
considerable number of the really ancient
works of Christian literature cannot read these
pieces without incidentally testing them in this
way to be genuine.

I did not seek these curious pieces out; they
were brought to me by students and others
who had come across them and wished information about them. As time went on I found
myself possessed of a number of them larger
than I, or I suppose anyone else, dreamed

PREFACE

FOR many years I have been engaged in the study of early Christian literature, a field in which the genuineness of every document must be rigorously investigated. In the course of this study, there have come to my attention, from time to time, from obscure private sources, writings claiming to be genuine documents of Christian antiquity. It was inevitable that I should instinctively test these stray pieces by the same tests that we constantly apply to all other documents supposedly ancient. In fact anyone familiar with any considerable number of the really ancient works of Christian literature cannot read these pieces without incidentally testing them in this way as he reads.

I did not seek these curious pieces out; they were brought to me by students and others who had come across them and wished information about them. As time went on I found myself possessed of a number of them larger than I, or I suppose anyone else, dreamed existed; so large a number in fact that it occurred to me that a useful service might be rendered by describing them together, and pointing out their failure to meet the simple and familiar tests of antiquity and genuineness.

They form a strange netful, dredged up from obscure depths mostly beyond the ken of educated people, and of little interest to them. Yet the mere collecting and describing of them may be useful, for while many people are acquainted with one or another of them, no one seems to know them all; and since there are undoubtedly others unknown to me, to list and test these eight may prepare the way for a fuller collection later.

Few of them have been discussed by scholars; they have for the most part been judged unworthy of serious consideration. And in one sense they are. But when a book is declared, as one of these has been, to be "next in importance to the Bible," and increasing numbers of people are being misled by it, it is time to put our fastidiousness aside and state the facts. Moreover the very bulk and number of them merit some attention, and since in the study of ancient literature we constantly seek to distinguish the genuine from the spurious, what is here gathered may at least serve as a footnote to the serious study of early Christian literature.

I am much indebted to Miss Maud Wilmot, of New Orleans, who called my attention to the Life of Issa, when it reappeared in 1926; to Dr. C. Wallace Petty, of Pittsburgh, who sent me a copy of one of the first American printings of it; to Professor Clayton R. Bowen, of Meadville Theological School, for many helpful suggestions and references; to Mr. Frederick W. Ashley, of the Library of Congress, for photostats of indispensable materials and for some very helpful letters; to Mr. W. A. Freidinger, of Suk el Garb, Syria, for invaluable information as to the "Confession of Pilate"; to Dr. Frank G. Lewis, of Crozer Theological Seminary, for photostats and letters relating to the "Report of Pilate"; to the late Professor John M. Coulter for bringing to my attention the Chicago edition of "The Crucifixion, by an Eye-Witness"; to Colonel T. A. Johnston, of Boonville, Missouri, for an enlightening interview; to my colleague, Professor Shirley J. Case, for a suggestion about the Essenes; to Professor J. M. Rife for information about the Greek form of the "Letter of Jesus Christ"; and to many members of my classes in early Christian literature who have helped to bring these documents together and to investigate them.

EDGAR J. GOODSPEED

September 4, 1930

CONTENTS

I

DISCOVERIES IN EARLY CHRISTIAN LITERATURE

⌣

THERE is a very natural and active interest on the part of almost everybody in any discovery that promises to throw light upon the beginnings and early years of Christianity, and especially upon the figure of Jesus. Nowhere is this interest more intense than among students of early Christian literature, and when a genuine discovery of some ancient Christian document really takes place, they are happier over it than anyone else. It is for such discoveries that they are constantly working and hoping, and such discoveries do now and then take place. The past fifty years have brought us the Teaching of the Twelve Apostles, the Gospel of Peter, the Revelation of Peter, the Apology of Aristides, the Acts of Paul, the Sayings of Jesus, the Odes of Solomon, and the Epistle of the Apostles—all from the second century.

But when this sincere concern is exploited and imposed upon by modern fictions masquerading as ancient works newly discovered, it becomes tragic business. One such pamphlet is now being circulated as a tract, envelope size, in a western state, at twenty cents a dozen. It has also been read over the radio Sunday evenings in one city of the Middle West as a religious exercise. It is now being republished in a book by a publisher who has been explicitly advised of its spurious character. Another has a place in the chapel service of an eastern school for girls. Another was laboriously copied on the typewriter and long circulated in carbon copies, which passed from hand to hand; one of these loaned me by an earnest Christian woman was my first introduction to the book.

What is to save our religious people from being duped by these hollow frauds? The application of the literary and historical tests which scholarship has worked out for judging ancient documents and documents supposedly ancient. There is nothing technical or intricate about these. They are no more than the application of experienced common sense, and can be followed and weighed by any intelligent reader.

The truth is, this yearning for new light on the dawn of the Christian faith is too fine and good a thing to be left a prey to charlatans and adventurers. It is easy for the learned world to disregard them as of no consequence, but meantime they are making an impression upon the untrained public which is often out of all proportion to their real value. A long series of letters and questions from earnest people who have heard of these things, and wondered about them, has led me to bring some of the more notable of them before the bar of scholarship, and ask what there is to be said for them, in the light of modern scholarly method.

It is the practice of scholars when any new discovery in ancient literature is brought to their attention to inquire as to the form in which it was found—the tablet, inscription, or manuscript from which it has been deciphered by its discoverer. What the scholar really desires is to see the very document itself, but failing that a photograph of it will usually answer the purposes of his investigation. He naturally wishes to scrutinize its material, whether papyrus, parchment, or paper; to examine the writing with an eye to determining its date; and in general to interrogate the discovery on a whole series of particulars bearing upon the all-important question of its genuineness.

If, however, even a photograph is out of the question, the scholar may for a time be content with a competent copy, made and vouched for by a capable and reputable scholar whose word cannot be doubted. But only for a time; and so clearly is this fact recognized by scholars that they usually lose no time in putting forth a photograph or sketch of any important discovery they may have claimed, so that it may make its own impression. At the very least they are usually quick to tell where the document in question is preserved, and to give every possible aid to other investigators who may be interested to verify their discovery.

For if the original cannot be shown, and a photograph of it is out of the question, the irreducible minimum upon which scholarship insists is exact information as to its whereabouts—the library, convent, or archive in which it lies, and the number, date, and other contents of the book that contains it. This is no caprice of learning, but a lesson learned by bitter experience of the overweening yearning of some people to be credited with discoveries that as a matter of fact were never made.

Many years ago a young German scholar of excellent promise announced that he had discovered three Greek fragments of Irenaeus, which he promptly published. They made him famous, which was probably what he desired. But he could never show the manuscript in which he had discovered them, nor direct anyone to it in any library. This gradually gave rise to a suspicion that there was no such manuscript, and this suspicion at length crystallized into a certainty. He had forged the fragments for the gratification it would give him to claim their discovery. This one sad incident makes it plain that if learning is to make sound progress in the discovery of ancient texts, every precaution must be taken to verify such claims.

This is even more true when such discoveries are reported by persons having no experience or technical skill in dealing with ancient documents, and hence liable to be deceived or imposed upon themselves. Whatever the source of the discovery, then, it is the business of scholarship to inquire most narrowly into its claims to acceptance, since only in this way can we hope to sift the genuine from the spurious. And every such claim must meet these tests if it is to have any right to the attention of intelligent or serious people.

When the manuscript or at least the original text has been shown and scrutinized, the next step is to search through ancient literature for any mention of the newly discovered work, or any sign of its use or influence. And finally the work itself must be studied in the light of our best knowledge of the thought and life of the times to which it claims to belong.

It is necessary to review this attitude and procedure of scholarship just now because recent years have witnessed the appearance of a whole flock of supposed discoveries of ancient documents, bearing upon the origin of Christianity and appealing especially to religious people, which have never been tested in this simple, fair, and natural fashion. Some of these have had a wide circulation.

The increasing frequency with which questions about these books have come to me and the absence of any sound and well-informed statement in print about most of them have led me to make these brief studies of their character and origin. In doing so I have been particularly struck with the way in which when assembled they seem to cancel and efface each other. Each one taken by itself may claim some slight plausibility, but when set side by side with half-a-dozen kindred fictions, any shadow of historical probability fades away. It is not without interest to try out our familiar methods of literary research upon works like these. They represent a certain type of naïve religious interest, not unknown in antiquity. Each presents a special problem to the investigator and has a curious interest of its own. Why should its author have composed it? What materials had he for his work? When and where did he do it? What success has it had?

But beside the intrinsic interest of tracing these fictions to their sources, there is I believe a practical need for some intelligent corrective for these mischievous little books. Many earnest people are being misled by their specious claims, which they are not in a position to test, for they circulate for the most part among groups far removed from scholarly circles.

Most of the little works dealt with in the following chapters have, it is true, been neglected by serious scholars, as so obviously fictitious as to call for no elaborate examination. Some of them, however, have attracted the attention of men like F. Max Müller of Oxford, Paul Schmiedel of Zurich, and Carl Schmidt of Berlin. But their work upon these documents is little known in this country, and at the best leaves the majority of the works treated in this book untouched. And it is one of the duties of scholarship to do what it can to protect the public against deception.

It may be that in taking the trouble to investigate them I seem to be taking them too seriously, and even to be extending their circulation. I should have no objection to such a a result. I have no ill-will to their authors or publishers, and no concern as to how widely these books circulate, provided their readers understand clearly what they are, and that they were written not in Alexandria and Jerusalem, but in Paris and Missouri.

There is finally the intellectual fascination of detection; of solving a live and novel problem; of unraveling a tangled skein; of unearthing the obscure origins of these pretentious fictions; and of showing ourselves superior to the arts of the impostor; and all this so convincingly as to satisfy if possible even the adherents of the books we have to treat. And no detective story would take the reader into more strange and far-off places than will this sober account of the actual origins of these curious works.

II

THE UNKNOWN LIFE
OF JESUS CHRIST

❧

IN THE summer of 1926 the newspapers in this country and abroad announced the discovery in a monastery in Tibet of a lost Life of Saint Issa, Best of the Sons of Men. The supposed discovery had, however, taken place nearly forty years before, and been published all over the world in 1894. The romantic story of its finding ran as follows:

In 1887 a Russian war-correspondent, Nicolas Notovitch, visited India, and proceeding into Tibet, at the Lamassary or Convent of Himis, learned of the Life of Saint Issa, Best of the Sons of Men. His story, with the text of the Life, was published in French in 1894 and passed through several editions that year. It enjoyed the widest publicity. It was translated into German, Spanish, and Italian. Three independent American translations were immediately published, two in New York and one in Chicago. The first (of The Life only) was by F. Marion Crawford, who was something of a Sanskrit scholar and had lived in India in his youth. It was published by Macmillan. Another English translation appeared in London in 1895.[1] The book called forth a vigorous controversy, attracting the attention of no less an authority than Professor F. Max Müller of Oxford. It was discussed at length in the pages of *The Nineteenth Century*, and then forgotten, until a New York publisher revived it in 1926, with the result described above.

Notovitch's account of his discovery of the work is that having been laid up by accident with a broken leg at the Convent of Himis, he

[1] "La vie inconnue de Jésus Christ" was published by Ollendorf in Paris in 1894. M. Henri Omont, of the Bibliothèque Nationale, informs me that at least eight editions of it were printed that year. Three separate translations of it, Mr. Frederick W. Ashley informs me, were entered for copyright at Washington in May of that year: on May 4, that of F. Marion Crawford, published by Macmillan; on May 18, that of J. H. Connelly and L. Landsberg, published by G. W. Dillingham, in New York; and on May 28, that of Alexina Loranger, published by Rand, McNally & Co., of Chicago. An Italian translation by R. Giovannini appeared the same year, and a German version, "Die Luecke im Leben Jesu," was printed in Stuttgart that year. A London translation, by Violet Crispe, published by Hutchinson, appeared in 1895. The Dillingham book was recently (1926) republished in New York by R. F. Fenno, but with copyright dated 1890! A Spanish version by A. G. de Araujo Jorge appeared in Rio de Janeiro in 1909.

prevailed upon the Chief Lama, who had told him of the existence of the work, to read to him, through an interpreter, the somewhat detached verses of the Tibetan version of the Life of Issa, which was said to have been translated from the Pali. Notovitch says that he himself afterward grouped the verses "in accordance with the requirements of the narrative." As published by Notovitch, the work consists of two hundred and forty-four short paragraphs, arranged in fourteen chapters. It begins with an account of Israel in Egypt, and its deliverance by Moses; its neglect of religion, and its conquest by the Romans. Then follows an account of the Incarnation. The divine youth, at thirteen, rather than take a wife, leaves his home to wander with a caravan of merchants to India (Sindh), to study the laws of the great Buddhas.

He is welcomed by the Jains, but leaves them to spend six years among the Brahmins, at Juggernaut, Benares, and other places, studying the Vedas, and teaching all castes alike. The Brahmins oppose him in this, and he denounces them and their sacred books, especially condemning caste and idolatry. When they plan to put him to death, he flees to the Buddhists, and spends six years among them, learning Pali and mastering their religious texts. He goes among the pagans, warning them against idolatry, and teaching a high morality, and then visits Persia and preaches to the Zoroastrians.

At twenty-nine Issa returns to his own country, and begins to preach. He visits Jerusalem, where Pilate is apprehensive about him. The Jewish leaders however find no fault in him, and he continues his work for three years, closely watched by Pilate's spies. He is finally arrested and put to death, not by Jewish influence, but through the hostility of Pilate. His followers were persecuted, but his disciples carried his message out over the world.

The interest of this little book is evidently to fill in the silent years of Jesus' youth, from the visit to Jerusalem at twelve to the beginning of his ministry at about thirty. It is interesting at the outset to observe that these two ages are taken for granted by the author of this work, who unconsciously bases his scheme upon them. We know them from the Gospel of Luke alone, and the question arises, Has the author of Issa obtained them from the same source?

It is also noteworthy that the work describes Jesus' ministry as three years in length, an idea derived from the Gospel of John, and from no other book of the New Testament. Had our author the Gospel of John as well as that of Luke? His emphasis upon the Incarnation shows that he had. Notovitch says that the Life of Issa was written within three or four years after the death of Christ, from the testimonies of eyewitnesses, and is hence more likely to bear the stamp of truth than the canonical gospels, which were written many years later. But the departure of the disciples to evangelize the pagan world, which is described in the last verse of the Life, did not take place within three or four years of Jesus' death. The idea that it did has probably been gained from the Gospel of Matthew, which, taken without the Acts of the Apostles, might suggest that impression. It looks as though the writer of the Life were acquainted with the Gospel of Matthew. Other touches point to his acquaintance with Acts and Romans, and it becomes clear that the range of Christian literature reflected in the book makes a date earlier than the second century impossible.

But this is only the beginning. The whole cast of the book is vague and elusive. It presents no difficulties, no problems, whereas any really ancient work newly discovered bristles with novelties and obscurities. The message of Jesus is a pallid and colorless morality, amiable and unobjectionable enough, but devoid of the flashes of insight and touches of genius that mark the early gospels. Historically and morally the book is commonplace. It identifies itself with no recognized type of primitive thought, and it does not strike out one of its own, but shows a superficial acquaintance with the leading New Testament ones, somewhat blurred together. This inaccurate acquaintance with the New Testament also characterizes Notovitch himself, who describes Luke as saying that Jesus "was in the deserts until the day of his showing unto Israel." This, he says, "conclusively proves that no one knew where the young man had gone, to so suddenly reappear sixteen years later" (p. 162). But it is not of Jesus but of John that Luke says this (1:80), so that it will hardly yield the conclusive proof Notovitch seeks. At this point in Luke's narrative, in fact, Jesus has not yet appeared.

On the whole, as an ancient document the Life of Issa is altogether unconvincing. It reads more like a journalistic effort to describe what might have happened if Jesus had visited India and Persia in his youth and what a modern cosmopolite thinks he did and taught in his ministry in Palestine.

The external evidence for the Life is no more impressive. The two large manuscript volumes read to Notovitch by the lama at the Himis Convent were, says Notovitch, "compiled from divers copies written in the Tibetan tongue, translated from rolls belonging to the Lassa library, and brought from India, Nepal, and Maghada two hundred years after Christ. These rolls were placed in a convent standing on Mount Marbour, near Lassa. . . . ." The rolls were written in the Pali tongue. It is evident that the scholar's desire to see the manuscript of the work, or failing that to see a photograph of it, or a part of it, or at least to have precise directions as to how and where to find it—its place and number in the Himis library—is not in this case to be satisfied. More than this, the Life of Issa does not purport to have been deciphered and translated by a competent scholar. The lama read, the interpreter translated, Notovitch took notes. He could evidently not control either the lama or the interpreter, to make sure of what the Tibetan manuscripts read. And his own notes, taken under these obvious disadvantages, he afterward spent many sleepless nights in classifying, "grouping the verses in conformity with the course of the narrative, and imprinting a character of unity to the entire work." Of course this is just what a scholar would not have done. He would wish to give the fragments just as the manuscripts had them, unaffected by his own views and tastes.

The Unknown Life attracted the attention of the great Orientalist Friedrich Max Müller, who in *The Nineteenth Century*[1] pointed out that the Life of Issa did not appear in the catalogue of the Tandjur and the Kandjur, the great collections of Tibetan literature. "If we understand M. Notovitch rightly," says Professor Max Müller, "this life of Christ was taken down from the mouths of some Jewish merchants who came to India immediately after the Crucifixion." He goes on to ask how these Jewish merchants happened, among the uncounted millions of India, to meet "the very people who had known Issa as a casual student

[1] "The Alleged Sojourn of Christ in India," *op. cit.*, XXXVI (1894), 515 f.

of Sanskrit and Pali in India, ... and still more how those who had known Issa as a simple student in India, saw at once that he was the same person who had been put to death under Pontius Pilate." He goes on to suggest that the Buddhist monks may have deceived Notovitch. "Two things in their account are impossible, or next to impossible. The first, that the Jews from Palestine who came to India in about 35 A.D. should have met the very people who had known Issa when he was a student at Benares; the second, that this Sûtra of Issa, composed in the first century of our era, should not have found a place either in the Kandjur or in the Tandjur."

If the monks did not indulge in duping Notovitch, nothing remained, Max Müller said, but to accuse M. Notovitch of a disgraceful fraud. And as he was writing his article, there came to him from an Englishwoman visiting Tibet a letter that pointed strongly in the latter direction. It was dated Leh, Ladakh, June 29, 1894, and read in part:

Yesterday we were at the great Himis monastery, the largest Buddhist monastery up here,—800 lamas. Did you hear of a Russian who could not gain admittance to the monastery in any way, but at last broke his leg outside and was taken in? His object was to copy a Buddhist life of Christ which is there. He says he got it and has published it since in French. There is not a single word of truth in the whole story! There has been no Russian here. No one has been taken into the Seminary for the past fifty years with a broken leg! There is no life of Christ there at all!

These and other criticisms Notovitch sought to answer in his preface to the London edition. "The truth indeed is," he remarks, "that the verses of which I give a translation in my book are probably not to be found in any kind of catalogue, either of the Tandjur or of the Kandjur.

"They are to be found scattered through more than one book without any title; consequently they could not be found in catalogues of Chinese or Tibetan works."

With these extraordinary observations the Life of Issa, Best of the Sons of Men, seems to evaporate and vanish away. For if its parts exist only thus scattered, the order and structure of the work are evidently the contribution of Notovitch himself, and the Life as a whole is his creation. This much he has admitted. Even now, a scholar would of course interest himself actively to secure copies and even photographs of the scattered portions which Notovitch says he has assembled. A work which makes such high claims would be well worth an expedition to Tibet, to search out the scattered verses, copy and translate them, and to provide an account of the documents in which they are imbedded. As it is, Notovitch seems to have taken refuge from his critics in a fog of indefiniteness. In his first preface he speaks of the monastic libraries as "containing a few copies of the manuscript in question," but now it is of no use to look for the manuscript, he intimates, for there is no manuscript, and he lightly refers serious students of his supposed discovery to "verses scattered through more than one book, without any title." This is not the method of sober scholarship. And we may observe that Notovitch himself in the thirty-five years that have elapsed since he published the Unknown Life has not taken the obvious and most of us would think the unavoidable steps to substantiate his supposed discovery. As a possible gesture in that direction we may quote his report in his London preface of a conversation with a Roman Catholic Cardinal, to whom he had mentioned the matter. "I may however add to what I have already said in my introduction as to having learnt from him that the Unknown Life of Jesus Christ is no novelty to the Roman Church, this: that the Vatican Library possesses sixty-three complete or incomplete manuscripts in various Oriental languages referring to this matter, which have been brought to Rome by missionaries from India, China, Egypt and Arabia." It is a thousand pities that the Cardinal, who had evidently counted the manuscripts, was not more explicit as to their titles, so that someone who could read them might have looked them up in that library. Even if Notovitch could not go back to Tibet to confirm his discovery, as he once boldly proposed to do, he might have reached Rome and found ample confirmation there. But in thirty-five years neither he nor his eight translators nor his nine publishers have been sufficiently interested to apply this very simple test. Nor has any independent student of the Vatican manuscripts reported one of the sixty-three manuscripts.

Some people have been harsh enough to say that Notovitch never visited Tibet at all. I am not in a position to say this. It is true that the pictures of Tibetan scenes and costumes

that appear in some editions of his work he
says are from photographs taken by his friend
D'Auvergne, who visited Tibet on another occasion. And I have observed that his accounts
of Tibetan buildings and practices bear a striking resemblance to some previously published
by English travelers. His account of his journey is not without improbability, and I cannot
learn that he is recognized among the serious
explorers who have visited Tibet. Yet he may
have gone there; it would obviously be difficult
to control his statement that he did.

Some light is thrown upon the matter by a
communication sent to *The Nineteenth Century*
in June, 1895, by Professor J. Archibald
Douglas of Agra, who was at that time a guest
in the Himis monastery, enjoying the hospi-
tality of that very chief lama who was supposed to have imparted the Unknown Life to
Notovitch. Professor Douglas found the ani-
mal life in the Sind Valley much less pic-
turesque than Notovitch had described, and no
memory of any foreigner with a broken leg
lingered at Leh or Himis. But Professor Douglas' inquiries did at length elicit the fact that a
Russian gentleman named Notovitch had
recently been treated for the toothache by the

medical officer of Leh Hospital. To that extent
Notovitch's narrative seems to have been on
firm ground.

But no further. The chief lama indignantly
repudiated the statements ascribed to him by
Notovitch, and declared that no traveler with
a broken leg had ever been nursed at the monastery. He stated with emphasis that no such
work as the Life of Issa was known in Tibet,
and that the statement that he had imparted
such a record to a traveler was a pure inven-
tion. When Notovitch's book was read to him
he exclaimed with indignation, "Lies, lies, lies,
nothing but lies!" The chief lama did not receive from Notovitch the presents Notovitch
reports having given him—the watch, the
alarm clock, and the thermometer. He did not
even know what a thermometer was. In short
the chief lama made a clean sweep of the representations of Notovitch, and with the aid of
Professor Douglas effected what Max Müller
described as his annihilation.[1]

In conclusion Max Müller expressly dis-
claimed any merit for having shown the Unknown Life to be a mere fiction, as no serious

[1] The Chief Lama of Himis on the alleged "Unknown Life of
Christ," *The Nineteenth Century*, XXXIX (1896), 667–78.

Sanskrit or Pali scholar, and no serious student of Buddhism, was taken in by it.

We may add that students of early Christian literature of course passed it by as of no significance whatever. It made no stir among them. This is not because they are averse to new discoveries. These are of frequent occurrence. But every one of them that is reported must stand the test of literary and textual criticism. To these tests the Life of Saint Issa, Best of the Sons of Men, fails to respond.

But it remains an interesting example of a whole series of modern attempts to impose upon the general public crude fictions under the guise of ancient documents lately discovered, and it is worth while to call attention to it because its recent republication in New York was hailed by the press as a new and important discovery.

III

THE AQUARIAN GOSPEL

❧

THE Aquarian Gospel takes its name from the fantastic astrological idea that with the life of Christ the sun entered the sign Pisces and that it is now passing into that of Aquarius. For the new Aquarian Age its author has composed a new spiritual gospel, the Aquarian Gospel. Its writer was Dr. Levi H. Dowling (1844–1911), who after years of service as chaplain, doctor, and Sunday-school worker became a believer in the Akashic Records, the imperishable records of life preserved in the Supreme Intelligence, or Universal Mind. By coming into harmony with the rhythms and vibrations of this, through meditation, Dr. Dowling, who preferred to be known simply as Levi, was able, he believed, to explore the past with unerring accuracy. The Aquarian Gospel is his record of the communications thus obtained and written down by him in California, in the "quiet hours," between two and six in the morning. It was published in Los Angeles in 1911.

The subjective character of materials gained in this way is to most of us immediately apparent. Yet the Aquarian Gospel has had a considerable circulation, and has found adherents in circles far removed from the half-theosophical atmosphere which produced it. I first saw it on the religious-books table of a large department store. It is, to begin with, arranged in sections, chapters, and verses. The chapters are preceded by brief summaries in italics, and each verse forms a little paragraph by itself, as in the King James Version. The distinctive readings of that version are occasionally recognizable in the Aquarian writer's use of the Bible.

"Augustus Caesar reigned and Herod Antipas was ruler in Jerusalem." This opening sentence of the new gospel does not encourage any very high hopes as to its historical value. It is generally accepted that Antipas never ruled in Jerusalem but in Galilee. Of course Dr. Dowling means Herod the Great. The first episode of the narrative is the birth of Mary to Joachim and Anna, her sojourn in the temple, and her marriage to Joseph. This is evidently derived from the ancient Gospel of James, or Protevangelium, a well-known work of early Christian literature. It is followed by accounts of the births of John and Jesus, drawn from Matthew and Luke. The location of Jesus' birthplace in a cave is another touch from the Gospel of James. The account of the martyrdom of Zacharias, which concludes this infancy section, is also drawn from that gospel.

This is followed by an account of the education of Mary and Elizabeth by Elihu and Salome, in Zoan. Their lessons dealt with the history of religions, and relate to Tao, Brahm, Zarathustra, and Buddha, the whole presentation being colored by Christian Science. The education of John by an Egyptian priest named Matheno is next described. This name recalls the famous Egyptian priest Manetho, who flourished early in the third century before Christ. Matheno was Master of a temple of the Brotherhood at "Sakara," and John spent eighteen years there with him.

But the education and travels of Jesus make up the most important part of the book. Jesus first studies with Hillel, then goes to India, where he spends years among the Brahmins and the Buddhists. He visits Tibet (Lassa, the

Ladakh, Leh), where he meets Meng-ste, the greatest sage of the farther East. This name suggests the Chinese sage Mencius (Meng-tsze), who died in 289 B.C. Everywhere Jesus learns the sacred books and talks with the greatest sages. He proceeds to Persia and visits the Magi, the chief of whom, Kaspar, welcomes and commends him. One is remind-ed that medieval legend gave this name, Gas-par, to one of the Magi mentioned in Matthew. Jesus passes through Assyria and Babylonia, reflecting on the life of Abraham and the Tow-er of Babel.

After a short visit to his home, Jesus goes to Greece, and preaches to the Athenians. He visits the Delphic oracle, which declares that its day is done. Jesus travels to Egypt, and joins the sacred brotherhood at Heliopolis. He passes through the seven degrees—Sincerity, Justice, Faith, Philanthropy, Heroism, Love Divine, and Christ—emerging as Logos. A council of the seven sages of the world is held at Alexandria. They formulate seven great re-ligious postulates, and ordain Jesus for his work.

There were undoubtedly great dramatic pos-sibilities in these situations, but the author of the Aquarian Gospel has not been equal to them. The contributions of the great ancient religions to truth might have been profoundly treated, but here they are no more than a theosophical jumble. The visits of Jesus to the Brahmins, Buddhists, and Persians remind us of Notovitch's "Unknown Life of Jesus Christ," with which Dr. Dowling was probably acquainted. But that idea is carried out much more systematically here.

The rest of the Aquarian Gospel is a fanciful recast of the materials of the Four Gospels, elaborated and diluted in Dr. Dowling's characteristic way. At the end, Jesus appears in a fully materialized body to friends in India, Persia, Jerusalem, Greece, Italy, Egypt, and Galilee. He declares himself to have been "transmuted to the image of the AM." A somewhat artificial vocabulary, now quaint, now pedantic, spoils the style of the book. Bizarre expressions like Holy Breath (for Holy Spirit), Christine (for Christian), the Septonate, the Triune God Father-Mother-Child, mingle with the technical terms of Christian Science and Theosophy in bewildering confusion. The simple piety and sound moral feeling that are on many pages are lost in the mass of fantastic yet artless fancies. The result is neither ancient nor modern. The principal impression is one of literary and religious commonplace.

The Unknown Life and the Aquarian Gospel have this in common, that they seek to fill in the hidden years of Jesus' youth; they seek in a measure at least to explain his wisdom by making him an adept in all that the older oriental religions had to give; and they put into their gospels what they like to think he did and taught. Notovitch has done this under this guise of a supposedly ancient document discovered by himself; Dowling, under the more transparent disguise of inner illumination.

IV

THE CRUCIFIXION OF JESUS, BY AN EYE-WITNESS

~

THIS is the story of Jesus as an Essene monk, destined for that order from his birth; of his ministry and Crucifixion; of his resuscitation and his lingering six months after in concealment among his Essene brethren, until his death. It is in the form of a letter written seven years after the Crucifixion, by an unnamed Essene elder at Jerusalem to one at Alexandria. It is controlled by a resuscitation theory of the Resurrection, and was written to present the gospel story stripped of all supernatural features.

Everything about the life of Jesus is here explained by the activity of his brethren of the Essene order. The angel of the annunciation who appeared to Mary was an Essene. It is even intimated that Jesus' father was an Essene. The flight into Egypt was directed by Essenes. John the Baptist was an Essene and

Jesus early became one. After the Crucifixion it was the Essenes who carried Jesus away and gradually revived him. Nicodemus was an Essene of the highest degree, and expert in the art of healing. The angel at the tomb was really an Essene, in the white robe of his order. Among the Essenes Jesus passed the remaining months of his life, occasionally showing himself to some of his followers. From the cradle to the grave Essenism surrounded him, and none but the Essenes possessed the secret of his life. The old story of his attachment for Mary of Bethany is retold, but he gives her up because as an Essene he must not marry.

The introduction states that the work was discovered in Latin in a parchment roll in an old Greek monastery in Alexandria. "A missionary," it proceeds, "in his fanatical orthodox eagerness tried to destroy the antique document." But it was saved and, in spite of Jesuit hostility, transcribed by a learned Frenchman, and a translation of it, into what language we are not told, but presumably into German, was brought to Germany by the Free Masons. The writer's interest in the Free Masons is very marked. He regards them as a survival of the Essene order, which in turn he traces back to the ancient Pythagoreans.

The German text was translated into Swedish, and the Swedish, in a "New Edition" (J. F. Sasberg, 1880), came into the hands of the Theosophical Society of Muskegon, Michigan, which produced this English translation.

The source of the text is explained in this note at the beginning of the book, written by Dr. Elsie Louise Morris, of Los Angeles, dated February 1, 1919: "In making copies of rare books and manuscripts in the Library of the Christian Israelites about fifteen years ago, I came across the MSS copy of this wonderful Letter of the Essene Elder in Jerusalem to his brother Elder in Alexandria, and copied it as accurately as I could. The treasured wisdom of this and similar libraries of this Order is not available for the public, and only accessible to advanced students for their private study and benefit, and not to be given broadcast to the world," as "only the initiated can properly interpret and use occult lore."

Dr. Morris does not tell us where this library is, nor what the manuscript's number is. In fact she does not make it clear in what lan-

guage she found it; but as her copy appears to
be the Muskegon theosophists' translation of
the Swedish version, it was evidently English.

Dr. Morris' note appears in the Los Angeles
edition, which bears no date, except that of the
copyright by B. F. Austin, 1919. But the book
had already been published in Chicago in
1907, by the Indo-American Book Company,
as Volume II of the "Supplemental Harmonic
Series." If Dr. Morris found the work fifteen
years before, that is, in 1904, it cannot have
been a copy of the Chicago edition of 1907 that
she saw. The explanation must be that the
Muskegon theosophists did not print their
translation but circulated it in typewritten
form, like the copy that was shown me in
Ames, Iowa, in 1926; that one of these copies
came to Dr. Morris' attention in 1904; and
another was published in Chicago in 1907;
and that in 1919 Dr. Morris turned her copy
over to Mr. Austin to publish in Los Angeles,
being either unaware that it had been already
published or else knowing that the book was
out of print.

The first point about the story to cause surprise is the parchment roll. Ancient manuscript rolls are of papyrus, not parchment.

Ancient parchments are in the form of leaf books, or codices. That one Essene should have written to another in Latin, before the middle of the first century, is also surprising. Aramaic we might have expected; even Greek we could have understood; but Latin goes against all the probabilities.

But let us assume that the Latin is an ancient translation of the Essene's original letter. The first inquiry scholarship would make would be for the Latin text. But the book before us gives us not a line of the Latin text, nor any hint of the present whereabouts of the manuscript itself—a matter of immense importance, if the supposed discovery is to be taken seriously. Yet the first translators of the work must first have copied the Latin text before they translated it; no one translates directly from an ancient manuscript without first copying its text. Nor have we any account of the size or date of the Latin parchment roll, or any hint of when it was found or of what has become of it. The statement that it was found by a "member of the Abyssinian Merchants Company" is also disturbing; fondness for humanistic research does not usually characterize the modern Abyssinian merchant.

We have in short neither (1) the manuscript, nor (2) a photograph of it, nor (3) directions for finding it for ourselves in some definite city or library, nor (4) a copy of its Latin text; no recognized expert in Latin manuscripts has seen and examined it; and so we are thrown back upon what is called internal evidence: the impression of authenticity and antiquity made by the translated document itself.

Although supposedly writing only seven years after Jesus' death, the writer has made much use of the Four Gospels. He actually refers to the gospels of Mark and Luke as already written, and reporting the Ascension,[1] but observes that John and Matthew did not record it; thus betraying an amount of acquaintance with the Four Gospels impossible only seven years after the Crucifixion, or at least thirty years before the earliest of them was written. Ignorance is as difficult to pretend as knowledge, and the author of "The Crucifixion" reveals by a hundred tokens his familiarity with characteristic features of the gospels. His very grouping of the four together

[1] As a matter of fact, neither Mark nor Luke in their earliest forms contained the Ascension, which crept into their text from Acts 1:9. See Westcott and Hort, "The New Testament in Greek," *in loco*.

points to a time more than a hundred years later than that at which he claims to be writing.

His acquaintance with the Gospel of John is conspicuous; sometimes he seems to be simply paraphrasing it. His occasional efforts to embellish its account are disastrous, as when he identifies Mary of Bethany with Mary of Magdala, describes the title over Jesus' head as written in four languages, and speaks of a "long cane of hyssop," evidently unaware that hyssop is a grassy plant that does not produce long canes.

The exclusion of every form of the supernatural from the story is another decidedly modern trait, very much out of place in the first century, when our modern scientific attitude of mind was of course unknown. And it is curious to find the persons mentioned strictly limited to those already familiar to us from the Four Gospels: "Warus"—doubtless meaning Varus, familiar from Josephus—is the only exception. Even the numerous Essenes introduced into the narrative in such profusion are left unnamed, not omitting the writer himself and the Alexandrian elder to whom he writes. In short we do not meet a single stranger in the whole narrative. This cannot be an accident.

That Jesus was an Essene seems to have been first suggested by Carl Bahrdt about 1784–92. It was later popularized by C. H. Venturini, 1800–1802, and has had many advocates since.

The picture of the Essenes as constantly in active touch with Jewish life, controlling and shaping it from behind the scenes, is altogether at variance with what we know of them from ancient sources.

The idea that Jesus did not really die upon the cross but was afterward resuscitated and so enabled to show himself at intervals to his disciples was advanced by early rationalists like Paulus and revived by Hase in his "History of Jesus" (*Geschichte Jesu*), in 1876. It may have been this book that occasioned the writing of "The Crucifixion, by an Eye-Witness." And finally the idea that Jesus cherished a romantic attachment for Mary, the sister of Lazarus, is a sentimental figment of nineteenth-century origin without a shadow of historical support. It is the crowning modern touch in a picture supposedly ancient.

To recapitulate: the use of the Four Gospels,

but no others; palpable blunders in the use even of them; inability to name any persons in the story except those mentioned in them; mistaken ideas about the Essenes; the introduction of the modern romantic interest; and the resolute rationalizing of the whole story, so alien to ancient modes of thought—these show at once that "The Crucifixion" is not the work of any eyewitness, as it professes to be, but of a nineteenth-century rationalist.

Tischendorf's brilliant manuscript discoveries in the Levant (culminating in his finding the Codex Sinaiticus in 1859) and the Egyptian romances of Ebers in the sixties and seventies might well suggest such a work as this, and explain the effort to put it forth as a genuine discovery of an ancient document, to which character it has not the slightest claim. Its purpose was of course to rewrite the gospel story stripped of the supernatural, an undertaking natural enough for the modern mind but altogether alien to the religious attitudes of the first century, Jewish, pagan, or Christian.

That the work is a translation from the German through the Swedish as it professes to be, is altogether likely. At some points the mean-

ing is hopelessly obscure, as though the translators themselves did not understand what was
meant. The obsolete word "muckender" (for
napkin), Warus (for Varus), Marcus, Lucas,
the Ephraimitical mountain (for Mount Ephraim), Bethania (for Bethany), the use of
Sopherim (scribes) as though it were a place,
reveal the translators as persons of no experience and very imperfect English culture. Frequent lapses in English (throwed, were tore, it
lays on the north, etc.) confirm this impression.[1] Here and there the Swedish version
clearly baffled the Muskegon translators. But
we must remember that they seem to have
planned simply a typewritten circulation for
their work, and not the wider and more pretentious printed editions which afterward appeared. The grave statement that the "true
transcript . . . . was saved from the orthodox
dumbhead" points at once to a German original and to a translator without a sense of
humor.

[1] Sentences like the following from the preface can only occur in a translation: "Under this period, the German translation of the Latin original was made public. Concerning the ancient discovered docu-ment, it consists of a letter from a so-called Therapute 'that is an elder' and in the highest degree of order standing fore-arm for the secret sciences, and the noble purposes which was the aim of the Essene Society" (p. 22).

The history of this curious work would therefore seem to be this: In the late seventies, some German, of strong Masonic sympathies, impressed by the novels of Ebers and the discoveries of Tischendorf, and influenced by the rationalistic views of the Resurrection recently revived by Hase, wrote "The Crucifixion, by an Eye-Witness" under the guise of a translation of a Latin work, discovered written on a parchment scroll in Alexandria. This was later translated into Swedish, and published in the seventies, for the "New Edition," connected with the name of J. F. Sasberg as publisher or editor, was dated 1880. This came, probably many years after, into the hands of the Muskegon theosophists, who produced and privately circulated a very crude translation of it. One copy of their work, about 1904, came to the attention of Dr. Morris, who copied, but did not publish, it. Another was printed in Chicago, in 1907, in a small volume of two hundred pages. In 1919 Dr. Morris showed her copy to Mr. Austin, who then published the Los Angeles edition.

V

PILATE'S COURT, AND THE
ARCHKO VOLUME

❧

IN 1879, the Rev. W. D. Mahan, a Cum-
berland Presbyterian minister, of Boonville, Missouri, published a pamphlet of
thirty-two pages, entitled "A Correct Transcript of Pilate's Court." It consisted chiefly
of an official report of the trial and death of
Jesus, made directly to the Emperor Tiberius,
by Pilate, as governor of Judea. Pilate describes his arrival in Jerusalem as governor,
the arrogance with which the Jewish leaders
treated his advances, his encounter with Jesus,
and the impression Jesus' words made upon
him. Pilate invites Jesus to an interview,
warns him of his danger from the Jews, and
urges him to be more moderate in his condem-
nation of them, but Jesus is unmoved. Herod
calls upon Pilate, and expresses his interest in
Jesus. At the Passover, an insurrection against
Pilate's authority broke out. Jesus was seized

by the rabble, brought before the high priest, and condemned to death. Caiaphas turned him over to Pilate for sentence and execution. As he was a Galilean, Pilate sent him to Herod, who again threw the responsibility upon Pilate. Pilate's wife, a Gaul of clairvoyant powers, warned him against harming Jesus. But he was carried away by the clamor of the mob, and unable with the few soldiers then at his command to assert his authority against the people, he washed his hands in disapproval, and allowed Jesus to be hurried away to crucifixion. Fearful portents and unnatural darkness attended his death. Joseph of Arimathea begged for his body, and placed it in a tomb. A few days later this was found empty, and the disciples declared that he was risen. Just as Pilate was finishing his report of the case to the Emperor, the night following "the fatal catastrophe," he heard the long-desired reinforcements, two thousand legionaries, marching to his relief—just too late to enable him to save Jesus.

Mr. Mahan accompanied this "Report" with a circumstantial account of how he came to know of the work and to become possessed of it. He stated that while he was living in

De Witt, Missouri, in 1856, a German scholar
named Henry C. Whydaman was icebound
there and spent several days at his house. In
the course of their conversations Mr. Whydaman told him of the existence of these "Acts of
Pilate" in the Vatican Library, and thought a
transcript of them could be obtained. Mr. Mahan became interested in the matter, and afterward, on September 22, 1856, he wrote Mr.
Whydaman for a copy of the text. Mr. Whydaman had returned to Germany, but answered from Westphalia, promising to do
what he could to secure one. Some months
later he wrote that Father Peter Freelinhusen,
the chief guardian of the Vatican, would provide a copy of the Latin text for thirty-five
darics, or sixty-two dollars and forty-two
cents. Mr. Mahan sent him a check on the
Foreign Exchange Bank of New York, and on
April 26, 1859, Mr. Whydaman's brother-in-
law, Mr. C. C. Vantberger, of New York, reported the arrival of the document, and offered
to translate it for ten dollars. Eight letters in
all are printed in explanation of how the document came into Mr. Mahan's hands. The
eighth is a letter from Father Freelinhusen to

Mr. Whydaman certifying to the accuracy of his copy of the Latin manuscript.

Mr. Mahan does not explain what he did with the "Report" during the twenty years that followed. But in 1879 he did at last publish it in the modest pamphlet above described. It seems to have met with gratifying success. Mr. Frederick W. Ashley, chief assistant librarian of the Library of Congress, informs me that it was republished within a year at Shelbyville, Indiana, by the Rev. George Sluter, A.M., who accompanied it with almost a hundred pages of introduction and notes, calling it "The Acta Pilati." In 1880 William Overton Clough republished it at Indianapolis, as the "Gesta Pilati." Mr. Clough went so far as to print several passages from it in Latin, but without saying whence he obtained the Latin form, and it must be admitted that the Latin has a very modern sound.[1]

There are obviously some grave difficulties

[1] This earliest form of the "Report," which appears in substantially identical form in the publications of Mahan, Sluter, and Clough, in 1879 and 1880, has recently been reissued in a mimeographed pamphlet, entitled "Pilate's Court," without date or place, except that the copyright for "Oregon and Washington Territory" is described as "owned by S. Monro Hubbard." The reference to "Washington Ter-

with Mr. Mahan's document and his story of
how he secured it. To begin with, the name of
Henry C. Whydaman does not have a German
ring. As Professor Schmiedel, the distinguished
scholar of Zurich, has since pointed out, Whydaman is no German name, and Westphalia is
not a place but a province. No such name as
Vantberger appears in the New York City
directories from 1853 to 1863, and the "Foreign Exchange Bank" does not appear among
New York banks of 1858. The name of Father
Peter Freelinhusen is unknown to the annals
of the Vatican Library. The use of darics in
Rome in the nineteenth century is a surprise
to most of us, who know that coin best from its
use in Xenophon's "Anabasis." It is noteworthy that Mr. Mahan had to have the document translated for him, though it was in a
language as well known as Latin. It is also
noteworthy that Father Freelinhusen made no
announcement of the discovery to the world of
scholarship, although the extraordinary importance of it, if it was genuine, could not
possibly have escaped him. The learned Mr.

---

ritory" seems to point to a date for this edition prior to 1889 when
Washington became a state. The form differs from Mahan's earliest
only in that the name of Pilate does not stand at the beginning.

Whydaman, who transmitted the Latin text to America, must have been aware of its importance, and even the mysterious Mr. Vantberger, of New York, should have known that the transaction left him possessed of a Latin text of extreme interest.

The misgivings raised by the story of how the "Report" was obtained are not relieved by the contents of the "Report" itself. The remark of Pilate that Herod "then reigned in Galilee" is a strange thing for Pilate to write to the Emperor the night after the Crucifixion; the Emperor must have known who was governing Galilee, and, as a matter of fact, Herod's tenure of office outlasted Pilate's. The excited words of Pilate's wife, "The statues of Caesar are filled with gemonide, the columns of the interium have given way," are certainly obscure. At this point, the translator, Mr. Vantberger, seems to have done his work very imperfectly. The crowd that hurries Jesus away to crucifixion utters such cries as "were never heard in the seditions of the panonia." The mob "streams out of the funeral gate leading to the Gemonica." This looks like an allusion to the Gemonian stairs at Rome. Dionysius the Areopagite, the Athenian mentioned in the

Acts, is in Jerusalem on the day of the Crucifixion. The picture of Jesus in his interview
with Pilate is romantic and theatrical, and the
Pilate reflected in the "Report" is historically
improbable. The whole work is a weak, crude
fancy, a jumble of high-sounding but meaning-
less words, and hardly worth serious criticism.
It is difficult to see how it could have deceived
anyone.

The strangest part of the story is that it did
deceive a great many people. Of course there
were some who immediately declared it a
fraud, but Mr. Mahan came boldly to the defense of his "Report" in advertisements and
letters to the Boonville paper.

The success of the "Report of Pilate" led
Mr. Mahan to further discoveries of the
same kind. In 1884, five years after the appearance of the "Report," he published a
considerable volume containing nine such
works, under the appalling title, "The Archaeological and the Historical Writings of the
Sanhedrin and Talmuds of the Jews, Translated from the Ancient Parchments and Scrolls
at Constantinople and the Vatican at Rome."
A series of letters at the beginning reports
visits made by Mr. Mahan first to Rome and

then to Constantinople, to study original sources for the life of Jesus. He secured the aid of two great scholars, otherwise unknown— Dr. Twyman, of England, and Dr. McIntosh, of Scotland. At the Vatican these three had no difficulty in seeing the manuscript of "Pilate's Report"; it was brought to them promptly the moment they called for it. They were thus able to expand Mr. Mahan's earlier form of it (which Father Freelinhusen had declared so exact) by about twelve hundred words, including a conclusion strongly resembling the corresponding part of the Gospel of Matthew, and ending with the inimitable words, "I am your most obedient servant, Pontius Pilate." The sad incident of the death from grief or fright, at the Crucifixion, of Balthasar, an aged and learned Jew of Antioch, now found a place in the "Report."

With "Pilate's Report" thus embellished were combined reports of interviews with the shepherds, Gamaliel's interview with Joseph and Mary, Caiaphas' reports to the Sanhedrin, Eli's story of the Magi, Herod Antipater's defense before the Senate for the slaughter of the innocents, and Herod Antipas' defense before the Senate—all with the claim that they were

copied and translated from ancient manuscripts in Rome or Constantinople.

Like the "Report of Pilate," these bristle
with childish blunders. There is no such Greek
philosopher and Roman legislator as "Meelee-
sen" (p. 6). The supposed references to Josephus' "Jewish Wars"—"Senect. 15, in brut.
15, quintil. 3 and 12"—simply do not exist.
That Josephus in his "Antiquities" refers to
Jesus in more than fifty places is false; the
supposed references given for finding these
have nothing to do with Josephus or Jesus;
they are "Suet. in dom. 13, Martial 9, v. 4."
The statements that Philo's works were translated into Greek by a Jewish rabbi named Si-
mon, that he often refers to Jesus, and that he
began to write about A.D. 40 are groundless; it
was at about that time that he ceased to write.
That Tacitus wrote his history of Agricola in
A.D. 56 is of course an error; Tacitus was born
in 55, and even if he had been able to write his
father-in-law's biography at the age of one
year, there was as yet nothing to write, for
Agricola himself was only nineteen. Mr. Mahan is not aware that the "Agricola" was written in Latin. He says it was translated by
Marcus, a Jewish rabbi; "and so were all the

histories written in this age. They were written in the languages of those days, and the scribes of those days were most all Rabbis." Mr. Mahan's statement that when Mohammed took Constantinople he had the fifty Bibles prepared for Constantine "all nicely cased and deposited in the St. Sophia Mosque" where "they look more like rolls of narrow carpet wound around a windlass than anything else" is baseless. Mr. Mahan thought that parchment was made out of vegetable pulp, reduced to a paste and dried in the sun, after which it was called papyrus! He gives no reference to manuscript numbers which might aid anyone to find and examine the books he claims to have found. The mention of Hilderium with Shammai and Hillel (p. 215) may be a reminiscence of Ilderim in "Ben-Hur"; there is no such Jewish name. As in "Ben-Hur," the Wise Men are a Greek, a Hindu, and an Egyptian. This with the story of Balthasar's death on the afternoon of the Crucifixion, which was absent from the original form of the "Report," had important consequences.

For Mr. Mahan's colleagues in the ministry were not slow to perceive his indebtedness, in Eli's "Story of the Magi," published in 1884, to "Ben-Hur," published in 1880. Chief among them was the Rev. James A. Quarles, then head of the Elizabeth Aull Seminary at Lexington, Missouri, and afterward professor in Washington and Lee University. Mr. Quarles was quick to observe that whole pages of Eli's "Story" were copied verbatim from "Ben-Hur." One detail that struck him with peculiar force was the mysterious word *anuman*, in this sentence: "Egypt is satisfied with her crocodiles and *anuman*, holding them in equal honor." On comparing this with "Ben-Hur," page 272, Mr. Quarles saw that Mr. Mahan in transcribing "Ben-Hur" had accidentally omitted a line. "Ben-Hur" reads:

Egypt was satisfied with her crocodiles and Anubis; the Persians were yet devoted to Ormuzd and Ahriman, holding them in equal honor;

which of course made everything plain.[1]

[1] A detailed comparison of Eli's "Story of the Magi" with' 'Ben-Hur" betrays Mr. Mahan's method and limitations. His strange reference (p. 121) to "the lawn of the Khan"—about the last thing anyone acquainted with a Syrian khan would expect—is explained by the mention in "Ben-Hur," p. 73, of "a lewen of the khan," in the very same connection: the Wise Men are resting there late at night. The description of the Virgin is also appropriated from "Ben-Hur," but her "drooping lids" are unhappily altered to "dropping" ones (from *ibid.*, p. 47). The freedom and extent of Mr. Mahan's copying of "Ben-Hur" are almost beyond belief.

Mr. Quarles attacked the genuineness of Mr. Mahan's discoveries in the *Boonville Weekly Advertiser*, with great keenness. He pointed out that Mr. Mahan was back in Boonville on November 6, 1883, although he claimed to have been discovering manuscripts in Constantinople on October 22, 1883.[1] We may add that the best opinion today in Boonville is that Mr. Mahan did not get farther away than Rome, Illinois, a little village north of Peoria, and that his foreign letters were dispatched from that place. He was absent from Boonville less than two months in the autumn in which he claimed to have visited Rome and Constantinople, discovering and copying manuscripts.

On November 13, 1884, Mr. Mahan answered Mr. Quarles, admitting that there were misprints in the book, but saying that he hoped to get "Lyman Abbot" to revise and enlarge it. "Even in its present condition," he goes on, "it is paying us about twenty dollars per day. . . . . You are bound to admit that the items in the book cant do any harm even if it were faulce, but will cause many to read and reflect that otherwise would not. So the

[1] Eli's "Story of the Magi," l. 2.

balance of good is in its favor, and as to the
truth of its MSS I stand ready to defend
them."

In his reply to this in the *Advertiser*, Mr.
Quarles said, February 14, 1885, "I assume the
responsibility of declaring that his nine manuscripts are, one and all of them, spurious."
Largely in consequence of his criticism, Mr.
Mahan was summoned before the Lebanon
presbytery in September, 1885, to answer
charges of falsehood and plagiarism.

In gathering evidence to lay before the presbytery, General Wallace, who was then American minister in Turkey, was consulted. The
matter is fully discussed in his "Autobiography," although it falls in the part of the
book written by Mrs. Wallace after the general's death.[1] General Wallace certified that no
such Hebrew manuscript of the "Story of the
Magi" as Mr. Mahan claimed to have used
was known to him, and further that no one
connected with the United States legation in
Constantinople in October, 1883, had any
knowledge of a visit of Mr. Mahan to the city,
nor could any of the American missionaries
about Constantinople, of whom General Wal-

---

[1] "Lew Wallace: An Autobiography" (1906), pp. 942-45.

lace had inquired, "recall at any time such a visitor to the capital, although few clergymen, especially those conducting such a research, ... stopped at Constantinople without making themselves known" (p. 943). "General Wallace received permission from the Sultan to visit the library" of the mosque of St. Sophia, in order to inquire for the manuscripts Mr. Mahan claimed he and Dr. McIntosh had found there. He was accompanied by Dr. Albert A. S. Long and others. "No book answering to the description given by Mr. Mahan was found, nor was there any trace of Hebrew manuscript in whole or in part relating to the story of the Magi. Zia Bey, the librarian, assured General Wallace that he had been in charge of the library for thirty years, and it contained no such manuscripts as Mr. Mahan professed to have seen." Dr. Long wrote to General Wallace confirming all this. "The librarian also certified that during his long incumbency of thirty years, but three or four parties besides that of General Wallace had visited the library, of whom he recalled the Emperor of Austria and the Empress Eugénie." It should be remembered that this investigation by General Wallace was under-

taken with all the prestige of a minister of the
United States, so extraordinarily popular with
the Sultan that when his term as minister ex-
pired the latter invited him to enter his service.
It was made within eighteen months of Mr.
Mahan's supposed visit to Constantinople and
the St. Sophia library, yet even then no one could
be found at the legation, at the library, at the
college, or among the missionaries who had
heard or seen anything of Mr. Mahan or Dr.
McIntosh. There is a strange irony in the fact
that at the very time when Mr. Mahan was
supposed to have visited Constantinople and
there to have read the story of the Magi from
an ancient manuscript, the author of that
story was residing there as United States
minister to Turkey.

In the light of this and of other evidence,
Mr. Mahan was found guilty of falsehood and
of plagiarism, and suspended from the ministry
for one year. He left the meeting of the presbytery, promising to withdraw the book from
circulation. But it was reprinted in St. Louis
in 1887, in Dalton, Georgia, in 1895, and in
Philadelphia, by the Antiquarian Book Company, in 1896. This edition had a strange se-
quel.

On August 1, 1898, the American minister to Turkey, James B. Angell, long president of the University of Michigan, reported to the Secretary of State that he had been asked by the Antiquarian Book Company to inquire whether the librarian at St. Sophia would supply a statement that the documents described in the book as found in the library of St. Sophia had been found there. Copies of the correspondence that followed have been sent me by Mr. Ashley. At the instance of Mr. Angell, the Turkish Minister of Public Instruction had taken the matter up, and on July 26, 1898, made the following report to Mr. Angell:

"From the investigations and examinations which have been made on the inquiries contained in the personal letter of His Excellency Mr. Angell, American Minister, it has been ascertained that neither the copy of any Bible ordered by the Emperor Constantine, nor any Report of Gamaliel on a conversation with the parents of Jesus, nor any report of Caiaphas on the crucifixion of Jesus, does exist in the Library of St. Sophia nor in any other of the libraries."

The representations of Mr. Mahan as to his discoveries in Constantinople have thus been

twice investigated in Constantinople by no
less a person than the American minister, and
with the same result. Nothing could be found
of the manuscripts he claimed to have seen
there.

A summary of this correspondence was published in the *Washington Star* of September 23,
1898, but the reprinting of the "Archko Volume," as it had come to be called, went steadi-
ly forward. It was republished in Topeka,
Kansas, as the "Archko Library," in 1904; and
in Philadelphia, as "The Archko Volume," in
1905. The "Autobiography" of General Wallace, with its exposure of Mr. Mahan's claims,
appeared in 1906, but did not affect the circulation and acceptance of the book. It made
its third appearance in Philadelphia in 1913,
and was reprinted in Chicago in 1923, by the
De Laurence Company, which does a large
mail-order business in charms, talismans, amu-
lets, and such things as most of us associate
with the Dark Ages. It has been printed more
than once in Grand Rapids, Michigan; most
recently (1929), in the face of serious protest,
by William B. Eerdmans. These are only a few
of its printings.

The original core of it all, the "Report of

Pilate," was republished in *Zion's Watch-tower*, Volume XIII (1892). It has also been translated into German and published apparently with some additions, at Barmen, Germany, for the "Ernste Bibelforscher," and a second German edition, 1919, attracted the critical attention of Professor Paul W. Schmiedel, of Zurich, who pointed out some of its manifest weaknesses in a tract entitled "Pilatus ueber Jesus bei den Ernsten Bibelforschern; Eine Faelschung entdeckt."

It was recently published as a tract, under the title "Letter of Pontius Pilate to Caesar," by the Free Tract Society, Inc., of Los Angeles, California, from whom it may be had at twenty cents per dozen. It was read over the radio from Davenport, Iowa, Sunday evenings in the summer and autumn of 1926, and the bulk of it was published in the *American Weekly Magazine* of December 4, 1927, with the statement that it was found in the Vatican Library in 1897.

What is the explanation of this curious story? The late seventies were the years when Colonel Robert G. Ingersoll was very much in the public eye, with his attacks upon the Bible. In 1876 he made his famous speech before the

Republican National Convention nominating
James G. Blaine for the presidency. In 1879
his lecture on "The Mistakes of Moses" was
published. Hundreds of men rose up to answer him, and a country preacher like Mr.
Mahan may well have felt stirred to help in
defending the Bible. The Book of Mormon had
appeared in 1830. The Mormons came to Missouri from Ohio in 1837, and settled in Cald-
well County, next to Carroll County, where
Mahan afterward lived. Knowledge of them
and their book may have contributed to his
strange writings. He perhaps knew something
of the amazing discoveries made by Tischendorf in the fifties in the libraries of the Levant.
The suggestion of a letter or report to the
Emperor doubtless came to him from the brief
apocryphal pieces of that kind translated by
Alexander Walker in the Edinburgh edition of
the Ante-Nicene Library, Volume XVI, which
appeared in 1873—the "Letter of Pontius
Pilate to Tiberius," the "Report of Pilate to
the Emperor Tiberius," and the "Acts of
Pilate," in the Gospel of Nicodemus. All three
of these titles—Letter, Report, Acts—have, it
will be observed, been applied to Mr. Mahan's
document. But the general color of his pam-

phlet is very different from those old fictions of
the fourth and fifth centuries, and often suggests the wild hysterical remorse of George
Croly's Wandering Jew "Salathiel," a book
better known in Mahan's day than now. It was
probably to establish for his document a date
prior to that of Walker's volume that Mahan
built up the elaborate Whydaman-Freelin-
husen-Vantberger correspondence with which
he prefaced it, which was meant to prove that
the "Report" had been in his possession since
1859.

At all events, in the late seventies, when
attacks on the Bible were most violent, this
uneducated man, fully convinced that such
documents as would support his views of it
must exist or have existed, saw no harm in
inventing a document calculated as he supposed to confirm the statements of the New
Testament as he understood it. Hardly had it
appeared in print (March, 1879) when in 1880
Lew Wallace's "Ben-Hur" made its sensational
appearance. This gave wings to Mr. Mahan's
imagination, and in 1884 "Pilate's Report"
has grown into the twelve chapters of the
"Archaeological and Historical Writings." He
writes without taste or skill; his unrefined

fancy sometimes descends to the vulgar and the indecent; his book is as Montague James calls it a "ridiculous and disgusting volume." Yet it has been printed and reprinted, however obscurely, in a dozen places, and actually welcomed as an aid to faith by earnest but uninformed people who should have been protected against such deception. The lesson is clear: We cannot dispense with the methods and resources of exact scholarship without exposing ourselves to pious frauds.

VI

THE CONFESSION OF
PONTIUS PILATE

~

THE "Confession of Pontius Pilate" tells the story of the arrival of Pilate as an exile, in Vienne, where he becomes the guest of his old friend Fabricius Albinus; of their conversation, and of Pilate's remorse and suicide.

"In the reign of Caligula, the Roman emperor," the narrative begins, "in the province of Roman Gaul (governed by Catius Marcius), four slaves in Jewish attire were one day leading an old gentleman of medium height, bent and greyheaded, his face denoting old age, his eyes, almost obscured by his heavy eyebrows, fixed to the ground." It proceeds to tell how Pilate in exile takes refuge with his friend Albinus, in the city of Vienne, where it will be remembered medieval tradition places the death of Pilate. In a series of conversations with Albinus, Pilate relates his chilling reception on his arrival in Jerusalem, and his impressions of the Jews, and of Jesus, for whose teachings he professes great respect. He tells how, to test his strength, Caiaphas planned a disturbance about Jesus, and brought him to Pilate for sentence and execution. The trials before Pilate and Herod followed, and in spite of Pilate's efforts on his behalf, Jesus was condemned and crucified. Dreadful portents attended his death. That night Pilate received much needed reinforcements of soldiers, arriving just too late to enable him to save Jesus. Two or three days afterward, Jesus' tomb was found empty.

The narrative continues with an account of Pilate's cruelties to the Jews, in revenge for their previous insults. Vitellius and Mary Magdalene accuse him before the Emperor Tiberius, and he is recalled to Rome. Before he arrives, Tiberius dies, and Caligula exiles Pilate to Vienne. All this Pilate relates to his old friend. Albinus condemns him for his conduct and after some discussion Pilate in despair throws himself from a mountain and dies.

This narrative was published in English by B. Shehadi, in New South Wales, in 1893, and reprinted in East Orange, New Jersey, in 1917.

The title-page describes it as "alleged to have been first written in Latin, by Fabricius Albinus," and "translated into Arabic by Jerasimus Jared, late Bishop of Zahleh, in Lebanon." The preface states that the Latin manuscript was discovered "early in the past century" in a cave near Vienne.

Inquiries about the bishop were directed to the Presbyterian Mission in the Lebanon and brought very gratifying results. Mr. W. A. Freidinger wrote me from Suk el Garb, in the Lebanon, in December, 1928, as follows:

"Jerasimus Jared, or rather Yarid, was a Greek orthodox bishop in Zahlah, Lebanon, Syria, some years ago, and he was known as a good man and friendly to all good causes. He was highly educated in the Russian language and did what writing he did in that language. It so happens that the Patriarch of the See of Antioch and his bishops are sitting in council in this Lebanon village at this time, and I asked the present Bishop of Zahlah for what he knew about the book, and he said that the book was originally composed by Bishop Gerasimus Yarid in the Russian language, and by him also translated into Arabic. This statement was made to me in the presence of other bishops and may be taken for the truth, I believe."

But in a subsequent letter to Mr. Freidinger, the bishop receded from this position, and stated that Bishop Gerasimus "took part of his story, translating freely, from a story he happened upon, in one of the foreign languages, but does not mention from which language." The Arabic editions of the work, which Mr. Freidinger kindly sent me, are dated 1889 and 1897, respectively.

The bishop's Arabic introduction, which is not included in the English version, contains these statements: "The story here set down is one we have wished published in the Arabic language. . . . . Part of this story is a free translation of a story we happened upon in one of the foreign languages, and it has come out suitable to the purpose in hand." The word "story" used here means a novel, romance, or fiction. Indeed the Arabic editions have a subtitle, "historical novel," after the main title, "The Confession of Pilate." It is therefore plain that the bishop made no historical claims for his work, such as his translator has assumed for him, but put it forth frankly for what it was—a modern fiction; and the omission of this candid little preface from the pen of the good bishop is a grave defect in the English version. It is plain that the present bishop gained his last impression about the origin of the "Confession" from a fresh examination of this preface.

It is still a fair question whether the bishop did not first compose the "Confession" in Russian, as his successor at first supposed. But careful inquiries kindly undertaken by Professor Bezobrazoff, of the Russian Theological Seminary in Paris, have failed to unearth any Russian form of it. Yet the bishop does very definitely claim some source for his work, as existing in a foreign language. What can this have been?

It is a very curious fact that while the general form of this narrative is unlike Mahan's "Report of Pilate," it presents a surprising number of striking agreements with that work, in details of fact and expression, which can only be explained by the dependence of one upon the other, or of both upon a common source. Whole blocks of Mahan's materials reappear in the "Confession." Mahan published his work ten years earlier than Bishop Gerasimus. If there is any direct dependence, it must be on the latter's part. It seems most improbable that an obscure pamphlet published in Missouri in 1879 should have found its way into the Lebanon and been used by a Greek Orthodox bishop in the eighties. The "Report" was certainly translated into German, and Mahan himself declared that a French scholar asked permission to translate it. But this was long after the publication of the Arabic "Confession." If the bishop knew the "Report," and it seems almost certain that he did, it must have been an English text of it that reached him. And it may have been the very "story" that he "happened upon in one of the foreign languages," as he says in his introduction.

But the "Confession" is in manner decidedly superior to the "Report," and with all its obvious shortcomings now and then reminds the reader of a sketch of Pilate written from a very different point of view by Anatole France, under the title "The Procurator of Judea." In that sketch France represents Pilate in later life as having completely forgotten the incident of Jesus' trial and death; even his name awakens no stir of memory. The "Confession," on the other hand, describes Pilate as haunted by the thought of his responsibility for Jesus' death, until it drives him at last to suicide. From the point of view of motive and interest, the two works are as far apart as possible.

Yet in many ways the "Confession" shows affinity with France's sketch. The general setting is much the same: Years after the Crucifixion Pilate meets an old friend; they talk of old times; meet again next day; dine together, and continue the conversation; discuss the Jews; Pilate declares that he was at first mild in his government of Judea, but expresses his conviction that the Jews must be "exterminated." He explains his removal from office as the work of Vitellius, who found a pretext in the Tirathaba incident, which each relates: France in the text, the bishop with less art in a footnote. The story was that a Samaritan claimed to have found where Moses had hidden the sacred vessels on Mount Gerizim, and a great number of people assembled to see them, when Pilate, suspecting a revolt, dispersed them with his soldiers, with much loss of life. In both works Pilate looks upon the Jews with great bitterness.

How is this resemblance to be explained? It is tempting to suppose that the bishop, seeing

France's sketch and resenting his very casual
references to Jesus, was stirred to write, with
materials drawn in large measure from the
Mahan "Report," an account of Pilate's remorse and death. But the "Confession" appeared in Arabic in 1889, while France's work,
ironically described as a Christmas story,
made its appearance in *Le Temps*, on December 25, 1891. We cannot suppose France was
influenced by an obscure Arabic booklet from
the Lebanon. The broad resemblance of the
two pieces must be due to the influence of some
other modern tale which chanced to come under the eye of both France and the bishop,
and from which the bishop drew his general
plan, while his substance he derived from
Mahan.

It is evidently quite unnecessary to make
any investigation of a document which, in its
original Arabic form, is frankly modern. The
story of Mary Magdalene presenting an Easter
egg dyed red to Tiberius (p. 38) would have
been enough to show that the "Confession" is
not earlier than the Middle Ages. The fourth-
or fifth-century Acts of Pilate, in some of its
forms, describes Mary Magdalene as saying,
"I will go alone to Rome unto Caesar; I will

show him what evil Pilate hath done, consenting unto the wicked Jews." Montague James remarks that the story of her going to Rome "appears in Byzantine chronicles and other late documents." Its diffuse and often sentimental character—as when Pilate is touched at the sight of a little girl—marks it as modern.

The English translator of the "Confession" has not only omitted the bishop's preface, but substituted one of his own. Misled by the *Encyclopaedia Britannica*, he states in this that according to Eusebius, Pilate committed suicide in Vienne about A.D. 38. But Eusebius says nothing about the place of Pilate's suicide; only a late tradition connects it with Vienne, to which place Eusebius says Antipas was banished. Even this is wrong, for it was Archelaus that was banished to Vienne; Antipas was banished to Lyons. We seem to have in the "Confession" a confusion between two late legends about the death of Pilate: one, that he was banished to Vienne; the other, that he committed suicide on Mount Pilatus near Lucerne. More ancient versions of his end are that he was beheaded by order of the Emperor, and that he killed himself with a knife, to escape execution.

But the "Confession" itself becomes immune to criticism the moment we observe that its original author put it forth frankly as a creation of his own. By publishing it in English without that acknowledgment, Shehadi has made it appear as an ancient historical document, to which status it has of course not the slightest claim.

VII

THE LETTER OF BENAN

IN 1910 there appeared at Berlin a work called *Der Benanbrief*, "The Letter of Benan," the Egyptian physician. It was described as translated from a Coptic papyrus roll of the fifth century, said to have been itself a translation of a Greek original written in A.D. 83. Its editor, Ernst Edler von der Planitz, stated that the roll was bought in 1860 by an independent Munich scholar named Baron von Rabenau, from a native in the village of Mit Rahinê, on the site of the ancient Memphis. It had been found in a tomb at Sakkara.

Von der Planitz went on to say that von Rabenau had put the four fragments together but had made only a mechanical word-for-word translation of them, when in 1877 he informed von der Planitz, then a youth of twenty, of the document, and after working on it fourteen years himself, decided to make the young man his assistant. Von Rabenau died in

1879, and von der Planitz describes himself as having worked thirty-four years on the text. As a result of their combined efforts a translation into modern form was produced, the plan being to accompany the letter with a full historical and scientific commentary. The result is five neat little volumes, the first two of which contain the translation; the third and fourth, notes on the text; and the fifth, a discussion of Jesus and his work in the light of "The Letter of Benan." It may be added that from one-fourth to one-third (or even two-fifths) of each volume is devoted to press notices and advertisements of von der Planitz and his works. The text is carefully divided into chapters and verses—long, numbered paragraphs, after the traditional Bible fashion.

The story is in brief as follows:

Benan, a priest of Memphis, writes to his friend Strato, once secretary to Tiberius, whom he had met when the eruption of Vesuvius found him in the amphitheater at Pompeii and drove him to escape to Capri in Pliny's galley. In conversation with Strato on that occasion, mention was made of the Christians. Benan told something of his early friendship with Jesus, and Strato told how Jesus' handkerchief, sent by Pilate's wife Procula, had cured Tiberius. (This recalls the legend of Veronica, and her handkerchief curing Tiberius.) Strato wished to hear more, but Benan had to sail for Egypt. Four years later, in A.D. 83, Strato is settled at Rhodes and writes to Benan to remind him of his promise to tell his story more fully. Benan's letter is the result.

Benan begins with the Wise Men and the star. Putiphra, an astronomer at Anu-Heliopolis in Egypt, is sent to the country of the Apriu (Hebrews) by the high priest Ranebchru, and discovers the star Siriu. At that very time a child is born there. The child is taken back to Anu and brought up by Ranebchru, being at the same time trained in rabbinic lore by Pinehas, the high priest of the Jewish temple of Onias near by. When he is twelve Putiphra dies and Jesus returns to Nazareth. He visits Jerusalem and amazes the scribes. But he soon returns to Leontopolis and Heliopolis, where he comes to know Benan, a youth who is studying to be a physician. Jesus also learns that art, and astonishes people with his cures. When Jesus is twenty-six he is visited by Philo; he has already become acquainted with the Therapeutae, a group of Essenes, who

practiced healing. Pinehas on his deathbed
charges Jesus to go to his native land as teach-
er and healer, and he goes. For three years no
news of him comes; then Asartis, a girl who is
in love with him, sends Benan to find him.
With another physician named Saites, Benan
goes, and on the way learns of Jesus' death.
Finding the crosses empty, the friends go to
the tomb and there witness the Resurrection,
of which they afterward inform the women
who come to the tomb. They also carry the
news of it to Bethany. Jesus appears again and
utters his lament over Jerusalem; then he
shows himself in Bethany, and finally calling
the disciples from Jerusalem, he commits to
them the preaching of the gospel and takes his
departure. Benan returns to Ranebchru in
Egypt with the news; the phoenix appears in
the temple of the sun at Heliopolis, in token of
the Resurrection, and Asartis dies of grief.

The second part of the letter tells of Benan's
subsequent journey to Italy, where he is unable
to help the dying Tiberius. But he becomes
the physician of Gaius and in that capacity
visits Gaul and Britain. Later he meets the
leading literary men of Rome, and witnesses the
burning of Rome in Nero's time, and the perse-

cution of the Christians that followed. Benan learns that their founder is his old friend Jehoshua, or Jesus, of Anu. Anxious to learn more of the sect, he visits Paul in his prison, and in that connection meets Seneca and Luke. Benan is involved in some way in Piso's conspiracy against Nero, and he accordingly flees from Rome to Antioch. He visits Nazareth and Jerusalem, where he meets James and the apostle John. After various adventures in connection with the outbreak of the Jewish war he takes refuge with Titus at Caesarea; becomes his physician; witnesses the fall of Jerusalem; follows his patron to Rome, and witnesses his triumph; intercedes successfully for the life of John, and is in the amphitheater at Pompeii witnessing the display of Christian martyrs when the eruption of Vesuvius drives him and Strato to Capri as already described.

Here again we see the interest in the "hidden years" of Jesus' youth, only in this case the main point is that Jesus spent his early years in Egypt becoming an adept in Egyptian priestly lore.

Some ten years later (1919) von der Planitz announced the discovery in a "public museum" (where, he does not say) of a Greek papyrus containing a reference to "Jesus of Anu," and thus confirming the truth of the account given in "The Letter of Benan." This attracted the attention of Professor Carl Schmidt of Berlin, distinguished for the discovery and decipherment of many early Christian Coptic pieces, and in an open letter he called upon von der Planitz to publish the original texts of both documents, the Coptic and the Greek. This was not done, but in a published statement von der Planitz answered Schmidt with great assurance and much bitterness. The attention that was by this time being given "The Letter of Benan" led Professor Schmidt to undertake a thoroughgoing exposure of its fictitious character, and he published in 1921 "The Letter of Benan, a Modern 'Life of Jesus' Fiction."[1]

Schmidt approaches "The Letter of Benan" with the fullest competence as a Coptic scholar, and a discoverer and decipherer of Greek and Coptic papyrus texts. His discovery and publication of the long-lost Acts of Paul in a Coptic version is but one of a series

[1] *Der Benanbrief, eine moderne Leben-Jesu-Faelschung*, "Texte und Untersuchungen zur Geschichte der altchristlichen Literatur," N.F., Vol. XLIV.

of achievements of his in this field, and it is fortunate that a man of his skill and learning has been willing to apply them to "The Benan Letter." He points out that in the first place von der Planitz is not a recognized Coptic scholar at all, but a writer of poems, novels, and stories, such as "The Lie of Mayerling," "The Full Truth about the Death of Crown Prince Rudolf of Austria," etc. To these we may add his more recent "In France as a Spy: A Chapter from My Life."[1]

Again, the Egyptologist von Rabenau, from whom von der Planitz obtained the text of the document, although von der Planitz describes him as a scholar of immense attainments, is a figure utterly unknown to German scholarship, which is all the stranger since as Schmidt remarks in the sixties and seventies the Egyptologists in Germany could be counted on one's fingers. And yet the account of this remarkable man is so precise and full that Schmidt is satisfied that some actual figure lies behind the name; and suggests that the portrait is drawn in the main from Professor Lauth of Munich, a very able and many-sided scholar of that very period, whose peculiar

[1] *Als Spion in Frankreich: Ein Kapitel aus meinem Leben* (1924).

views and conjectures are often reflected in
von der Planitz' book, and whose erratic and
fanciful positions finally separated him from
the more temperate scholarship of his day.
Lauth was at Munich in von der Planitz'
student days there: he died in 1895, at the age
of seventy-three.

Further, the Coptic manuscript is said to
have been a roll. But Coptic literary manuscripts are never rolls, but always leaf books—
codices. Moreover the "Letter" occupies two
hundred and thirty printed pages and would
have been vastly too long for any practical
Greek or Coptic roll, which were seldom more
than six or seven yards in length.

that's a long letter

The dialect, too, is said to have been Mem-
phitic (that is, Bohairic—the dialect of the
Delta district). But there were no Coptic
translations in that dialect at that early date;
our earliest Bohairic manuscripts are centuries
later.

The "Letter" is, moreover, a jumble of
Egyptian, Greek, Latin, and Hebrew words
and even phrases such as was never found in
an ancient Coptic papyrus.

That the handkerchief in the Veronica
legend was used by Jesus on his way to cruci-

fixion is a development of the fourteenth- or
fifteenth-century forms of that legend.

These and many other points of greater detail are convincingly urged by Schmidt against
the genuineness of the "Letter." Of special importance is the disappearance of the manuscript itself, which was lost sight of after the
death of von Rabenau in 1879. It is strange
that whoever came into possession of it at that
time has never mentioned it, nor has it ever
come to light at all. Even more strange is the
failure of von der Planitz to publish a photograph or facsimile of it, or even a transcript of
its Coptic text, of which he nevertheless seems
to possess a copy, for he claims to have worked
over it for thirty-four years, and in his two
volumes of notes on the "Letter" often refers
to the text. For the whole thing, so immensely
important, if genuine, we have only the word
of a publicist of no standing as an expert in
Coptic, who cannot show his manuscript or
even a copy of the text he claims to publish.
The external, or manuscript, evidence is therefore very disappointing.

The internal evidence has already been
shown to be extremely unfavorable. The reader will observe that the time of its supposed

discovery was the period of Ebers' Egyptian romances; "An Egyptian Princess" appeared in 1864, and "Uarda" in 1877. The name Benan is that of the second of the Hyksos kings of Egypt, as Lauth once misread it. Ranebchru is another of Lauth's mistakes, a misreading of the name of an Eleventh Dynasty monarch. Pinehas, the high priest, recalls Phinehas the high priest of Exodus and I Chronicles. The Jewish temple at Leontopolis is the one described in Josephus. Jesus' boyhood visit to Jerusalem is that described by Luke. That Jesus learned magic in Egypt was suggested by Celsus before the end of the second century. Philo's interest in the Therapeutae can be gathered from the work "On the Contemplative Life" usually ascribed to him. The three-year ministry of Jesus in Palestine shows the influence of the Gospel of John.

The other gospels (all four of which von der Planitz assigns to the second century!) have influenced the account of the Resurrection appearances. The phoenix as a symbol of the Resurrection is mentioned in the Letter of Clement of Rome to the Corinthians, A.D. 95, usually called I Clement. The burning of Rome, the persecution of the Christians, and the reference to Piso's conspiracy recall the accounts in Tacitus, and the visit to Paul in his prison shows the influence of Acts. The connection of Seneca with Paul's circle shows acquaintance with the well-known but spurious correspondence between them. The Jewish war, the fall of Jerusalem, and the triumph of Titus show the influence of Josephus. The fourth-century Abgar legend and the Veronica legend in its latest—fourteenth- or fifteenth-century—form are used. And finally the amphitheater scene at Pompeii brings us into the familiar atmosphere not so much of Pliny's letters about Vesuvius as of Bulwer-Lytton's "Last Days of Pompeii" (1834). Where else is a spectacle of martyred Christians in the Pompeii amphitheater made the prelude to the great eruption of Vesuvius?

The striking thing about all this is that one man should have succeeded in participating in so many of the great events and scenes of his day—the Resurrection of Jesus, the death of Tiberius, the burning of Rome, the first persecution, the imprisonment of Paul, the fall of Jerusalem, the triumph of Titus, the trial of John, the eruption of Vesuvius, and so on. It is of course clear that such a series of personal adventures is not autobiography but fiction, and fiction based for the most part upon familiar sources.

In general then and in detail, "The Letter of Benan" upon examination betrays itself as a product of the imagination, and it is a pity that its writer did not content himself with putting it forth as such, instead of making this absurd pretense of genuineness and antiquity for it and surrounding it with a vast mass of notes designed to impose upon the uninformed.

VIII

THE TWENTY-NINTH CHAPTER
OF ACTS

❧

FOR many years there has prevailed in certain quarters in England the idea that the Anglo-Saxon peoples are the lost ten tribes of Israel who were carried into captivity by Assyria in 722 B.C., and have never been heard of since. The holders of this "British-Israel" position declare that the national seal of the United States bears witness to our identity with the tribe of Manasseh, the thirteenth tribe (Gen. 49:24, Hos. 14:6, etc.), while the royal arms of Britain recall those of Ephraim and Judah (Gen. 49:9, Deut. 33:17, etc.). George Washington and King George V are both in fact lineal descendants of King David.

The starting-point of these identifications is the Old Testament prophecy of a great future for the chosen people and an enduring dynasty for David's line; David should never want a

man to sit upon the throne of the house of
Israel (Jer. 33:17, 20, 21). When Jerusalem fell
into the hands of the Babylonians Jeremiah
escaped with the daughters of Zedekiah the
king to Egypt (Jer. 43:6, 7). This must have
been about 586 B.C. What became of these
princesses? Irish legend declares that about
580 B.C. an eastern princess of great beauty
accompanied by a prophet or seer was shipwrecked on the northeast coast of Ireland.
The king of Ulster married her, and they were
crowned together on a "Stone of Destiny"
which the prophet had brought with him. This
coronation stone, the Lia-Fail, the British-
Israel school maintains was afterward taken to
Scotland, and thence as the Stone of Scone to
England, where to this day the kings are
crowned seated upon it. And these kings are
the descendants of the shipwrecked princess
who escaped from Jerusalem with Jeremiah
after the conquest of Judah by Nebuchad-
nezzar. Indeed the British-Israelites declare
that the Princess Tea Tephi lies buried under
the sacred hill of Tara and that some day when
her tomb is opened the Ark of the Covenant
may be found buried with her.

One of their most interesting claims is the

discovery of the twenty-ninth chapter of the Acts of the Apostles.

This "long-lost chapter of the Acts of the Apostles, containing the account of Paul's journey in Spain and Britain" is said by a recent publisher of it, Mr. T. G. Cole, to have been translated by the oriental traveler, C. S. Sonnini, from a "Greek manuscript found in the Archives at Constantinople, and presented to him by the Sultan Abdoul Achmet." Sonnini's translation, we are further informed, "was found interleaved in a copy of Sonnini's "Travels in Turkey and Greece," and purchased at the sale of the library and effects of the late Right Hon. Sir John Newport, Bart., in Ireland, ... in whose possession it had been for more than thirty years, with a copy of the firman of the Sultan of Turkey, granting to C. S. Sonnini permission to travel in all parts of the Ottoman dominions."

The copy of Sonnini's "Travels" in which it was found was an English translation, printed in London in 1801, under the title, "Travels in Turkey and Greece Undertaken by Order of Louis XVI, and with the Authority of the Ottoman Court." The original French edition appeared in Paris in the same year, but con-

tains no allusion to any such gift from the
Sultan. The English text of the new chapter
of Acts is said to have been published by Ste-
venson in London in 1871. I have found no
earlier date given for it.

The disposition of the British-Israel group to
find theology, chronology, and prophecy in the
dimensions and passages of the Great Pyramid
recalls the efforts in that direction made by the
British astronomer Charles Piazzi Smyth, who
published "Our Inheritance in the Great Pyramid" in 1864, and "Life and Work at the
Great Pyramid" in 1867. The association of
his views with the British-Israel movement
makes it natural to connect the composition of
this additional chapter of Acts with that
time.

The chapter continues the narrative of the
Acts with an account of how Paul departed
from Rome (his imprisonment seems to create
no difficulty) for Spain and Britain, "for he
had heard in Phoenicia that certain of the
children of Israel, about the time of the Assyrian captivity, had escaped by sea to the isles
afar off, as spoken by the prophet, and called
by the Romans Britain." Paul accordingly visits Spain, and preaches there with much suc-

cess. He then proceeds to Britain, landing at Raphinus (believed to be Sandwich in Kent). He preaches on Mount Lud (the future site of St. Paul's Cathedral) and confers with the Druids, who reveal their descent from. the Jews "who escaped from bondage in the land of Egypt." He then travels through Gaul and preaches to the Belgians. In Switzerland he visits Mount Pontius Pilate, where Pilate "dashed himself down headlong and so miserably perished." He goes on, by way of "Mount Julius" (the Julian Alps between Italy and Austria), to Illyricum, on his way to Macedonia and Asia—with the evident intention of writing the Pastoral letters, Timothy and Titus.

The text as recently published in London (by the Covenant Publishing Company), and also in Toronto, has a curious interest:

1. And Paul, full of the blessings of Christ, and abounding in the spirit, departed out of Rome, determining to go into Spain, for he had a long time purposed to journey thitherward, and was minded also to go from thence into Britain.

2. For he had heard in Phoenicia that certain of the children of Israel, about the time of the Assyrian captivity, had escaped by sea to the "isles afar off," as

spoken by the prophet, and called by the Romans Britain.

3. And the Lord commanded the gospel to be preached far hence to the Gentiles, and to the lost sheep of the house of Israel.

4. And no man hindered Paul; for he testified boldly of Jesus before the tribunes and among the people; and he took with him certain of the brethren which abode with him at Rome, and they took shipping at Ostium, and having the winds fair were brought safely into an haven of Spain.

5. And much people were gathered together from the towns and villages, and the hill country, for they had heard of the conversion of the apostle, and the many miracles which he had wrought.

6. And Paul preached mightily in Spain, and great multitudes believed and were converted, for they perceived he was an apostle sent from God.

7. And they departed out of Spain, and Paul and his company finding a ship in Armorica sailing unto Britain, they went therein, and passing along the South coast they reached a port called Raphinus.

8. Now when it was noised abroad that the apostle had landed on their coast, great multitudes of the inhabitants met him, and they treated Paul courteously, and he entered in at the east gate of their city, and lodged in the house of an Hebrew and one of his own nation.

9. And on the morrow he came and stood upon Mount Lud; and the people thronged at the gate, and assembled in the Broadway, and he preached Christ

unto them, and many believed the word and the testimony of Jesus.

10. And at even the Holy Ghost fell upon Paul, and
he prophesied, saying Behold, in the last days the God
of peace shall dwell in the cities, and the inhabitants
thereof shall be numbered; and in the seventh number-
ing of the people, their eyes shall be opened, and the
glory of their inheritance shine forth before them. And
nations shall come up to worship on the mount that
testifieth of the patience and long suffering of a servant
of the Lord.

11. And in the latter days new tidings of the gospel
shall issue forth out of Jerusalem, and the hearts of the
people shall rejoice, and behold fountains shall be
opened, and there shall be no more plague.

12. In those days there shall be wars and rumors of
wars; and a king shall rise up, and his sword shall be for
the healing of the nations, and his peacemaking shall
abide, and the glory of his kingdom a wonder among
princes.

13. And it came to pass that certain of the Druids
came unto Paul privately, and showed by their rites and
ceremonies they were descended from the Jews which
escaped from bondage in the land of Egypt, and the
apostle believed these things, and he gave them the kiss
of peace.

14. And Paul abode in his lodgings three months,
confirming in the faith and preaching Christ continually.

15. And after these things Paul and his brethren departed from Raphinus and sailed unto Atium in Gaul.

16. And Paul preached in the Roman garrisons and among the people, exhorting all men to repent and confess their sins.

17. And there came to him certain of the Belgae to inquire of him of the new doctrine and of the man Jesus; and Paul opened his heart unto them, and told them all things that had befallen him, how be it that Christ came into the world to save sinners; and they departed, pondering among themselves upon the things which they had heard.

18. And after much preaching and toil, Paul and his fellow labourers passed into Helvetia, and came unto Mount Pontius Pilate, where he who condemned the Lord Jesus dashed himself down headlong, and so miserably perished.

19. And immediately a torrent gushed out of the mountain, and washed his body broken in pieces into a lake.

20. And Paul stretched forth his hands upon the water, and prayed unto the Lord, saying, O Lord God, give a sign unto all nations that here Pontius Pilate, which condemned thine only-begotten Son, plunged down headlong into the pit.

21. And while Paul was yet speaking, behold there came a great earthquake, and the face of the waters was changed, and the form of the lake like unto the Son of Man hanging in an agony upon the cross.

22. And a voice came out of heaven saying, Even Pilate hath escaped the wrath to come, for he washed his hands before the multitude at the bloodshedding of the Lord Jesus.

23. When therefore Paul and those that were with him saw the earthquake, and heard the voice of the angel, they glorified God, and were mightily strengthened in the spirit.

24. And they journeyed and came to Mount Julius, where stood two pillars, one on the right hand and one on the left hand, erected by Caesar Augustus.

25. And Paul, filled with the Holy Ghost, stood up between the two pillars, saying, Men and brethren, these stones which ye see this day shall testify of my journey hence; and verily I say, they shall remain until the outpouring of the spirit upon all nations, neither shall the way be hindered throughout all generations.

26. And they went forth and came unto Illyricum, intending to go by Macedonia into Asia, and grace was found in all the churches; and they prospered and had peace. Amen.

We have already seen, in discussing the "Confession of Pontius Pilate," that the story of his suicide on Mount Pilatus is a late legend. The researches of General Wallace and President Angell at Constantinople have shown that no such manuscripts as are here implied are known in the libraries there. On the other hand no manuscript of the Acts in Greek or any other tongue contains the chapter, and the conclusion is unavoidable that it was composed to support the British-Israel movement which circulates it. The testimony of the

Druids in verse 13, and Paul's prophecy of
St. Paul's Cathedral and of the seventh
British census of 1861, and the rise of the
British-Israel movement soon after, verse 10,
show this interest unmistakably.

That the original Greek of this chapter was
given to Sonnini by the Sultan has no support
from Sonnini's book of travels, according to
which he did not even see the Sultan, but secured his permission to travel, through others.

The fantastic legend that the Lake of Lucerne assumed its present shape, faintly sug-
gesting a crucifix, on the occasion of Paul's
visit there (p. 21) is altogether unlike the
writer of Acts, especially the part of his work
that deals with Paul.

The reference to Pilate's washing his hands
at the time of Jesus' trial (vs. 22) would be
strangely out of place in Acts, the author of
which does not mention it in his account of the
trial (Luke 23). The words "men and brethren" (vs. 25) reflect an old mistranslation of a
Greek phrase in Acts, now generally corrected;
and the expression "Verily I say," here put
(vs. 25) into the mouth of Paul, is one never
used by Luke, and rigidly reserved by Matthew and John ("Verily, verily I say") for

Jesus alone. To use it of Paul is most unlike the New Testament.

In view of its interest in the British census of 1861 (vs. 10), and the popularity given to ideas of this kind by the work of Piazzi Smyth in the sixties of the last century, it is probable that this curious chapter was written not long before its publication in 1871.

IX

THE LETTER OF JESUS CHRIST

✦

THE particular interest that called forth each of these curious works has already been indicated in connection with each. Publicity, rationalism, traditionalism, piety, avarice—are all represented. The old forces that produced apocrypha are still at work. Not long ago, the newspapers reported the discovery at Cerignola in Italy of an ancient gospel written in Greek on thirty-one sheets of parchment. The manuscript was in a hand of the third or fourth century, but the work was composed by Joseph or Josephus of Jerusalem, who was supposed to be no other than our old friend Josephus. It was said that a certain Signor Moccia had bought from a Roman antiquary an antique wrought-iron casket which proved to have a false bottom. Under this was found the manuscript. There was much talk of a rich American's intention to purchase the thing, when Signor Moccia's associate in the matter, Signor Gino Gardella, came forward with a statement that it was all a fiction, which he and Moccia had produced with the best of intentions, in the hope of stimulating faith. The whole affair was really no more than a publicity scheme designed to advertise a forthcoming novel by Moccia, but was abandoned by its projectors when they saw how seriously it was being taken.

In 1894 Catulle Mendès, a French literary man, published a new infancy gospel under the title *L'Évangile de la jeunesse de Notre-Seigneur Jésus-Christ d'après S. Pierre*, "The Gospel of the Childhood of Our Lord Jesus Christ according to St. Peter." The French text was accompanied by a supposed Latin original, which was said to have been found some years before in the Abbey of St. Wolfgang in the Salzkammergut. Ten years later it appeared in English, under the title "The Childhood of Christ, Translated from the Latin by Henry Copley Greene." It has been described by Provost Montague James as a sentimentalized compilation from the Protevangelium of James, the Gospel of Pseudo-Matthew (of the eighth or ninth century), the Latin Gospel of Thomas, and the Arabic Gospel of the Infancy. Its relation to the last of these, as Dr. James points out, is especially instructive. The Arabic Gospel was first published by Sike in 1697 from an Arabic manuscript which has since disappeared. But many phrases from Sike's Latin translation of it appear in the supposedly original Latin of this new infancy gospel from Paris. It is evidently a modern work, and was probably composed by Catulle Mendès himself, who to give it an air of authenticity translated it into Latin.

Of still another sort is a little volume of "Letters of Pontius Pilate," recently published (1928) by W. P. Crozier. These thirty-three short letters are represented as written by Pilate to Seneca between the years 26 and 30. While the editor represents them as genuine, it is soon clear that this is simply a thin disguise for a purely imaginative sketch of Pilate's experiences and moods during the opening years of his government of Judea. This is so manifest that no serious attention has been paid to them.

Very similar to these are the "Letters from Pontius Pilate's Wife," recently published by Catherine van Dyke (October, 1929). They are described as "rewritten from an old traditional manuscript first found in a monastery at Bruges, where it had lain for centuries." All that we really know about Pilate's wife is what is said of her in Matt. 27:19, but this has intensely interested both ancient and modern readers in her. There is something very human and moving in the glimpse of this highly placed woman trying to mitigate the brutality of Roman government, and one cannot help wondering whether she did not make similar efforts on other such occasions. Her supposed letters, like those of Pilate just mentioned, are unmistakable pieces of historical fiction.

This is also the case with what purported to be another ancient letter, newly discovered—the "Epistle of Kallikrates," published in the *Atlantic Monthly* for March, 1928. This was the answer of one of Paul's Corinthian converts to Paul's letter known to us as I Corinthians, and sought to show the practical difficulties in the way of acting upon Paul's instructions in that letter. But a few minutes' examination of the letter was enough to show that the reaction was a modern, not an ancient one, and so obvious was this that the antiquity and authenticity of the "Epistle" were hardly anywhere even broached. Everyone saw at once that its pseudonymity was simply a device for getting a hearing for a modern thinker's sense of the difficulty of applying Paul's teaching in I Corinthians to modern situations.

The most ambitious and yet the most commonplace of modern apocrypha is probably the "Letter of Jesus Christ," said to have been found under a stone near Iconium, where it was deposited by the angel Gabriel. It is sometimes sent through the mail with a request that the recipient send copies of it to three others, as some great misfortune is likely to befall him if he does not. "Do not break the chain." It was published almost in full some years ago in the *Chicago Evening Post*, and is sometimes found framed on the walls of people of more piety than intelligence.

It consists principally of some artless precepts about attending church and observing the Sabbath, but its text has been so often debased by inaccurate reprinting that it is sometimes difficult to make out just what the original meant to say. I have not been able to learn anything about its age or author, but it seems to have originated in England, forty or more years ago, for the framed form of it is

pressmarked at the end, "Pitts—— Great St.
Andrew St. Seven Dials.—One Penny."[1]

Montague James says the "Letter" is "extant in almost every European language and in many Oriental versions. It was fabled to have fallen on the altar at Jerusalem, Rome, Constantinople—where not?"

Three sources for the text of the letter are before me: a printing of it in the *Chicago Evening Post* of May 16, 1917; a copy made from a framed text of it which a friend of mine found hanging on the wall of a house he visited, and kindly copied for me; and a tract printed in Chicago, November 17, 1917, and peddled from door to door. To the student of text-transmission, whether ancient or modern, the variations which have crept into the text of this obscure tract are highly instructive. They show just that disposition to ramble into interpolation and paraphrase which marks one well-known and very primitive type of New Testament Greek text, and supply a valuable hint for its explanation. For this tract has been often copied and reprinted quite unofficially and

[1] This English printing contains also the fourth-century correspondence between Jesus and Abgar, king of Edessa, and the (probably medieval) "Letter of Lentulus," about the personal appearance of Jesus.

without ecclesiastical or scholarly supervision, by persons irresponsible and untrained, yet pious and well meaning. In just such ways of course many New Testament books were copied and recopied, in the second and third centuries, in circles beyond learned or official control.

The text as gathered from these three sources is as follows:

"A copy of a letter written by our blessed Lord and Saviour Jesus Christ, and found eighteen miles from Iconium sixty five years after his crucifixion; transmitted from the Holy City by a converted Jew; faithfully translated from the original Hebrew copy, now in the possession of the Lady Cubasse's family in Mesopotamia. This letter was written by Jesus Christ, and found under a stone large and round, at the foot of the cross. Upon the stone was engraven, 'Blessed be he that shall turn me over.' All people that saw it prayed to God earnestly and desired that he would make this writing known to them, that they might not attempt in vain to turn it over. In the meantime there came out a little child about six or seven years of age, and turned it over without assistance, to the admiration of every person who was standing by. Under this stone was found the following, written by Jesus Christ. It was carried to the city of Iconium, and there published by a person belonging to the Lady Cubasse. On the letter was written: 'The Commandments of Jesus Christ; Signed by the Angel Gabriel ninety nine years after our Saviour's birth.'

"Whosoever worketh on the Sabbath day shall be cursed. I command you to go to church and keep the Lord's day holy, without any manner of work. You shall not idle or misspend your time in bedecking yourself with superfluities, costly apparel and vain dressing, for I have ordained it a day of rest. I will have that day kept holy, that your sins may be forgiven you.

"You shall not break my commandments but observe and keep them, they being written by my own hand and spoken with my own mouth. You shall not only go to church yourself, but also your man servants and your maid servants. Observe my words and learn my commandments. You shall finish your labour every Saturday in the afternoon by six o'clock, at which hour the preparation for the Sabbath begins.

"I advise you to fast five days in the year, beginning with Good Friday and continuing the four Fridays following, in remembrance of the five bloody wounds I received for you and all mankind.

"You shall diligently and peaceably labour in your respective callings wherein it has pleased God to call you. You shall love one another and cause them that are not baptized to come to church and receive the holy sacraments, baptism and the Lord's Supper, and to be made members of the church. In so doing, I will give you long life and many blessings; your land shall be replenished and bring forth abundance. I will comfort you in the greatest temptations, and surely he that doeth to the contrary shall be cursed. I will also send hardness of heart upon them until I have consumed them, especially upon hardened and impenitent unbelievers.

"He that hath given to the poor shall not be unprofited. Remember to keep holy the Sabbath day, for the seventh day have I taken as a resting day to myself.

"He that hath a copy of this letter, written with my own hand and spoken with my own mouth, and keepeth it without publishing it to others, shall not prosper, but he that publisheth it to others shall be blessed of me. And if their sins be in number as the stars of the sky and they truly believe in me, they shall be pardoned. And if they believe not this writing and my commandments, I will send my plagues upon them, and consume both you and your children.

"Whosoever shall have a copy of this letter and keep it in their house, nothing shall hurt them, and if any woman be in child-birth and put her trust in me, she shall be delivered of her child. You shall hear no more of me but by the Holy Spirit until the Day of Judgment. All goodness and prosperity shall be in the house where a copy of this letter shall be found."

Few people, it is to be hoped, could be imposed upon by a document so crudely unhistorical as this; yet even it has had its public on both sides of the Atlantic. Somewhat akin to it is "A Letter of our Lord Jesus Christ, Found on the Grave of the Mother of God," a much longer tract now current in modern Greek and published by Michael Saliveros, in Athens. In this, the letter is revealed when Joannicius, patriarch of Jerusalem, smote a stone that had fallen from heaven. This Greek form of the letter is much more violent and denunciatory than the English forms given above. It is also much more extended. The common elements of the two forms are enough, however, to make it pretty certain that one is a development from the other, and if that be true, the Greek represents the elaborated form and the English the more primitive. Probably the patriarch, finding the shorter, milder form, developed it into the savage tirade which we find in the Greek.

These pages have shown that the amount of this modern apocryphal literature is much larger than anyone has suspected, and the popularity and influence of some of these pieces are simply amazing. We have heard much of late of the unmasking of modern impostures in the field of sculpture and of painting. I have seen a whole book devoted to spurious Egyptian antiques. There is undoubtedly a widespread disposition to play upon the universal esteem for the classical or the antique. It is in fact a very real tribute to the worth of the genuine documents of Christian antiquity that men should still be striving to produce imitations of them now. And it is I believe our business as intelligent people to know the imitations as well as the genuine, especially as many people of limited education are being so imposed upon.

I have also had a feeling that these documents when brought together in a measure nullify one another, being so palpably efforts to employ the same literary devices for contradictory purposes. And it may throw the genuine writings of primitive Christianity into higher relief to see these imitations in their true character.

INDEX